IMAGES
*of America*

# NEWPORT

This photograph of fishing vessels docked at Newport, Oregon, was taken August 28, 1931. Until about 1912, few fishermen crossed the Yaquina Bay bar to fish. Most of the fishing was done in the bays and rivers. Once equipped with gasoline engines, fishing vessels were able to fish in the open ocean on a regular basis. The number of commercial fishermen based in Newport grew substantially in the late 1920s and early 1930s as large canneries and processing plants, equipped with improvements in refrigeration and transportation, began locating in the area. (LCHS No. 1142.)

ON THE COVER: Miss Newport, Beverly Jean Duncan, sits at the tip of the bow (with her back to the camera) of the charter vessel Spotlight. She is celebrating with other contestants, dignitaries, and friends on Sunday, May 18, 1948, the official "Miss Newport Day," proclaimed by the city of Newport that year. (LCHS No. 2230.)

IMAGES
*of America*

# NEWPORT

Diane Disse, Jodi Weeber, Loretta Harrison,
Lincoln County Historical Society

ARCADIA
PUBLISHING

Published by Arcadia Publishing
Charleston, South Carolina


Library of Congress Control Number: 2010928310

For all general information, please contact Arcadia Publishing:
Telephone 843-853-2070
Fax 843-853-0044
E-mail sales@arcadiapublishing.com
For customer service and orders:
Toll-Free 1-888-313-2665

Visit us on the Internet at www.arcadiapublishing.com

*This book is dedicated to the men and women who recognized the need to preserve the history of Newport and Lincoln County, Oregon, for future generations. In 1948, they formed the Lincoln County Historical Society, which today administers two museums and provides numerous programs.*

*The first board of directors included: Mark Brooks, president; Alice Rush, vice president; L. W. Rakes, secretary; Ada May Smith, treasurer; and directors J. R. Edwards, Paul Van de Velde, and Jim Howes.*

# CONTENTS

# ACKNOWLEDGMENTS

To say that history is always changing begs the question of whether there is a fundamental truth that can be discovered or whether we are dependent on many voices and perspectives to allow us to present a document as history. The latter allows us to attempt to give a snapshot in the present of a time in the past, and that is what the writers have done here, with a photographic emphasis.

The photographs come from the collection of the Lincoln County Historical Society, which has benefitted from the generosity of many donors—from the formation of the society in 1948 to the present. Some of the individual collections were particularly helpful, including those of A. L. Thomas and Roger A. Hart.

The information comes from a number of invaluable sources, including Richard Price's *Newport, Oregon 1866–1936: Portrait of a Coastal Resort*, Steve Wyatt's *Bayfront*, and numerous other publications. Invaluable information also came from the many files and documents of the research library of the Lincoln County Historical Society.

The entire project was supported by the Lincoln County Historical Society and its dedicated board of directors, staff, and volunteers, who devote their time and energy to making the museums and other programs work, and by the people of Lincoln County, who support the society through their county government. Members and visitors make up the extended family of support and also earn the society's appreciation.

Finally, the writers would like to pay homage to the people whose stories are told through these photographs—the people who helped make Newport and Lincoln County, Oregon, what it is today.

# INTRODUCTION

The story of Newport, Oregon, is a tale about natural resources and the people who make a living from these natural resources. Early tribal groups lived strictly off the bounty of the river, the bay, and the flora and fauna, moving from area to area to follow the seasons of the harvest. The first recorded landing at Yaquina Bay by outsiders occurred after the Revolutionary War had already begun, when Capt. James Cook anchored offshore with his ships *Resolution* and *Discovery* in 1778.

Before settlers found the area's hidden resources, the U.S. government considered the area uninhabitable and, in 1855, designated it part of a reservation for 4,000 people from about 20 different coastal, southern Oregon, and northern California tribes.

The discovery by outsiders of a rare oyster, the *ostrea lurida*, in Yaquina Bay brought companies from San Francisco to harvest the oyster, leading to pressure to open up the land around the bay to settlement. In 1866, the land now known as Newport and areas adjacent to it were removed from the reservation. Settlers staked their claims immediately.

Among those first settlers was Sam Case, a volunteer soldier sent to the reservation. Case stayed after the Civil War to work on the reservation and lobby the government to open the area around Yaquina Bay to settlement. Case chose a prime spot where Yaquina Bay meets the ocean. There he built a resort hotel like those he had seen while vacationing in Newport, Rhode Island, and on July 4, 1866, named the town "Newport" and the hotel "Ocean House." Other settlers started a sawmill, worked in the oyster business, and started fishing and shipping ventures. Retail businesses came soon after.

Development spread out from Newport and the Ocean House on all sides. In the late 1800s and early 1900s, tourism took a tighter hold, and the Nye Beach area began to develop with hotels, hot sea baths, a theater, a miniature golf course, agate shops, and many other attractions.

One natural resource, spruce trees, brought a dramatic change to the area during World War I. The army created a spruce division to harvest the lightweight wood for use in airplane construction. The infrastructure they built became the foundation for a thriving milling industry that remains today. The war also made it clear that transporting people and materials along Oregon's coast was unreliable. Construction of the Roosevelt Military Highway (now Highway 101) helped improve transportation and make the area friendly to the increasing automobile traffic.

The Depression brought many changes to the area also, as the National Recovery Act carried out projects, including parks, schools, and the Yaquina Bay Bridge. Until completion of the bridge, along with a bridge over Alsea Bay, it was not possible to travel the length of the Oregon coast without being ferried across water.

World War II brought with it the realization that even on the far western coast, we were vulnerable to attack. It was the beginning of a true realization of the importance of Yaquina Bay and Newport.

# One

# NATIVE TRIBES

Yaquina Bay and the land around it on the central Oregon coast have been inhabited by humans for at least 5,000 years, perhaps longer than 8,000 years. Verification of the presence of prehistoric humans has been accomplished mainly through carbon dating, using contents of the shell middens and ancient house pits at Yaquina Head, Seal Rock, and Whale Cove. Middens are heaps of shells, bones, and tools left by ancient people who camped and worked close to the ocean. The house pits positioned nearby show their wares.

The latest native tribe to inhabit the area, the Yacona, lived on the Oregon coast from 1400 AD or earlier. The Yacona traveled seasonally from place to place to search for food. Middens indicate where they fished, gathered mollusks, and hunted sea lions and seals.

After contact with outsiders, life changed dramatically for the Yacona and nearby tribes. Illness and conflict reduced the population. After the Rogue River Wars, about 4,000 natives from 20 different tribes were placed on the Coast Reservation, which opened in 1855. The central portion of the reservation, including the area now known as Newport, opened to settlement in 1866, and the southern and extreme northern portions opened in 1875. Most of the remaining land was allotted to reservation residents in 1892. In 1954, the Confederated Tribes of the Siletz Indians was terminated by an act of Congress; all remaining Siletz lands, except for the 39 acres known as Government Hill, were sold. Government Hill was given to the city of Siletz.

In the late 1960s, a core group of tribal members began work to revitalize common bonds. They restored the tribal cemetery on Government Hill and developed programs to provide job training and social services and began lobbying Congress and the president to again recognize the Siletz as a federal Native American tribe. In 1977, the federal government restored tribal status, and the Confederated Tribes of the Siletz was formed.

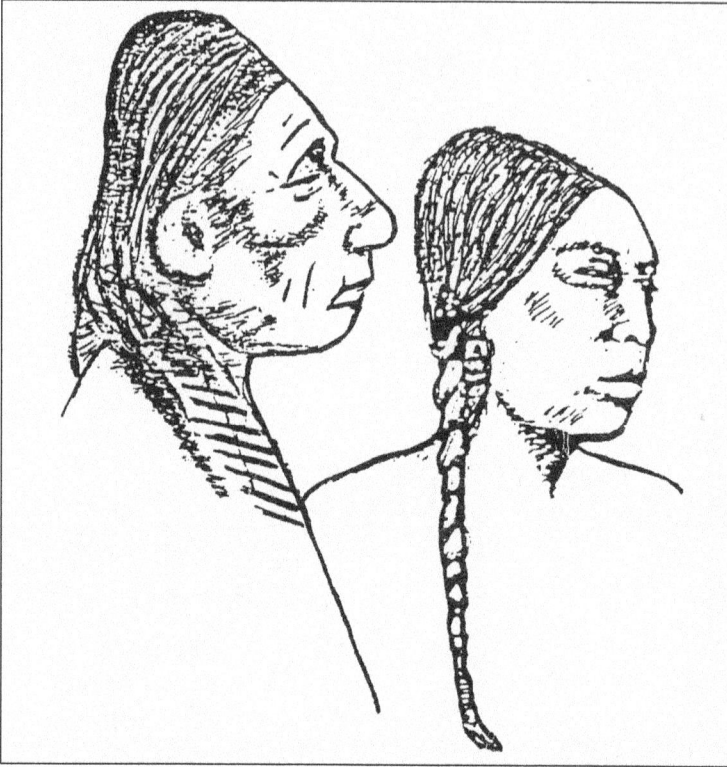

The Yacona, who inhabited the Yaquina River area around approximately 1400 AD, had dark skin and brown eyes. The Yacona flattened babies' heads during the first months of their life so that they would be distinguished from other tribes in the afterlife. When Lt. Theodore Talbot explored the area in 1849, he found only about 85 living Yacona, their population decimated by disease and forest fires. (Drawing from *The Indians of Yaquina Bay*, E. Wayne Courtney.)

Much of the information on early inhabitants comes from studying the items they discarded, including shells, bones, and tools. Shell mounds, such as those pictured here in Yachats, are referred to as middens. Many of these shell mounds have been destroyed or altered by road and highway construction and scavenging. The locations of remaining middens often are kept secret to preserve their integrity. (LCHS No. 2248.)

10

In 1861, the Civil War broke out, and volunteer soldiers replaced trained soldiers at the Coast Reservation. About that same time, companies from San Francisco came to Yaquina Bay to harvest a rare and delicate oyster found there. Pressure from these newcomers led to the opening of 200,000 acres around Yaquina Bay to white settlement in 1866. The order divided the Coast Reservation into a southern, or Alsea, portion and a northern, or Siletz, portion. Oysterville, pictured here about 1890, was created by the oyster-harvesting companies. The companies used Native Americans living on the reservation in the harvesting, including Annie Ditallo, known as the "Rock Oyster Queen." (Above, LCHS No. 346; right, LCHS No. 1195.)

"ROCK OYSTER QUEEN" NEWPORT, OREGON.

Buildings were constructed for administering the reservation. Tribal children were placed in a boarding school to teach them European ways and compel them to give up their tribal traditions and language. The school is second from right in the early 1900s photograph of Government Hill, the name given to the site of the agency buildings. In 1892, the General Allotment Act took effect at Siletz. Parcels of about 80 acres each were allotted to the 551 remaining tribal members. Except for five timbered sections reserved for the use of reservation residents, the remainder of the reservation was opened to homesteading in 1894. Siletz Agency workers are pictured in this 1892 photograph below. Only Willard L. Linville, clerk, (behind the desk) is identified. (Above, LCHS No. 1841; below, LCHS No. 1849.)

The reservation operated a store where Native Americans could purchase items and trade their goods. In 1881, James Chambers was named post trader. He died a year later, leaving his wife, Clarinda, with four children, debts, and the store. Clarinda applied for and was granted a license to be the post trader. She was the first woman to receive such a license. Clarinda later married Clark Copeland. (Above, LCHS No. 1846; below, license from files of LCHS.)

The federal government designated the Methodist denomination to care for the souls of the Native Americans, and a church was built on Government Hill. This photograph of the Methodist congregation was taken in 1927. Other religions also vied for the spiritual lives of the Native Americans, including St. Mary's Catholic Church in Siletz, pictured below in 1897 with some of its congregants. (Above, LCHS No. 501; below, LCHS No. 2249.)

Indian Camp, Newport, Oregon.

At Yaquina Head, the sea mussel was the most common mollusk used by the Native Americans. Nearly a fourth of the Yacona diet consisted of fish, almost nine percent birds, and approximately three percent marine and forest mammals. The forest fauna they consumed were mainly deer and elk. Marine animals included two species of sea lions, the northern fur seal, whales, and sea otters. Even after the reservation was closed, Native Americans continued to camp, hunt, and fish, as seen in the camp pictured here. Annie Miner Peterson (below), like many other tribal people, also continued to practice longtime skills, such as basket weaving. (Above, LCHS No. 1028; below, LCHS No. 1041.)

Many early settlers married Native American women, including George Megginson, who was hired by the reservation to supervise farming ventures by the natives. In the 1870s, George and his wife, Julia, moved to a homestead that included today's Agate Beach and the location of Yaquina Head Lighthouse, which opened in 1873. Many generations of Native American families became part of the Yaquina Bay community, including the five generations pictured below, about 1909, of Molly Carmichael, Jane Yanna, Maime Strong, Mary Catfish, and baby Stanley Strong. (Left, LCHS No. 1379; below, LCHS No. 1513.)

Native Americans from the Siletz Reservation (or Coast Reservation) participated in many activities on Yaquina Bay, including a parade to Nye Beach in 1901. (LCHS No. 34.)

Native Americans from the Siletz Reservation performed a dance on the Bayfront by the Abbey House about 1912. (LCHS No. 2250.)

# Two

# THE EARLY YEARS OF SETTLEMENT

When Yaquina Bay was opened to settlement in January 1866, soldiers, trappers, oystermen, and other adventurers were waiting to claim the free land. Single men could claim 160 acres, married men 320.

Sam Case, a soldier on the reservation, claimed the northwest end of the Bayfront; Fred Olsson, who had come to harvest oysters, claimed adjacent land to the east that became known as Olssonville; and John Nye staked his claim to a 160-acre parcel that reached from Case's claim west to the ocean.

Case envisioned a resort town at the mouth of Yaquina Bay and set about building the Ocean House. At an 1866 Independence Day celebration, the town was named Newport after Newport, Rhode Island, a resort town Case had visited. A year later, Newport, which then referred only to Case's land on the Bayfront, had two stores, two hotels, two saloons, one restaurant, one copper shop, two fish packing plants, and one meat market. By 1868, Sam Case was teaching at the first school in Newport. Some fathers worked on the road to Elk City to pay their children's tuition.

By 1869, shipping was picking up, and an independent schooner line was formed, with San Francisco as the biggest market and Portland the main competitor. To aid shipping ventures, Yaquina Bay Lighthouse opened in 1871. It operated fewer than three years when it was decommissioned and a new lighthouse opened at Yaquina Head, a more strategic location. In 1881, the federal government appropriated money to build a jetty on the south side of Yaquina Bay. In 1896, the U.S. Life Saving Service, a precursor to the Coast Guard, established a station at South Beach on Yaquina Bay. It was there until 1906.

The railroad came to Yaquina Bay in 1884 but not all the way to Newport. It ended at Yaquina City, a town built upriver by the developers of the railroad. As the coastal settlements grew, residents wanted more local control, and in 1893, Lincoln County was formed from parts of Benton and Tillamook Counties.

In 1863, Capt. Solomon Dodge established a base for Winant and Company to harvest rare oysters on Yaquina Bay. Richard Hillyer arrived soon after, representing Ludlow and Company. Reservation agent Ben Simpson protested the harvesting of oysters on reservation lands without compensating the natives. Simpson established that right in a legal battle, and Winant and Company agreed to pay for taking oysters, while Ludlow and Company refused. James J. Winant, pictured here prior to 1889, developed his base into a small settlement with a store and lodging for the oyster harvesters. (LCHS No. 1762.)

Mary Hall Sturtevant arrived in Oysterville in 1865 with her new husband who had come to harvest oysters. She was thought to be the first white woman to live on the Coast Reservation. Mary's husband abused her, and she divorced him. Soon after, she married Royal Bensell, a soldier on the reservation who had stayed and started the area's first sawmill. (LCHS No. 2251.)

This is the oldest known photograph of the Bayfront, probably taken in the mid-1860s. Both whites and Native Americans are pictured in the photograph, which shows Livingston's Cake and Beer and Butch Hammer's Card and Whiskey Saloon. (LCHS No. 934.)

Barges, such as those pictured here around 1890, were used to harvest oysters. The native oysters were depleted by 1880 because of overharvesting, but harvesting continued with the descendants of a transplanted Asian species that flourishes in the bay. (LCHS No. 1350.)

Fishing was an early venture on Yaquina Bay, with abundant catches taken in small rowboats like these around 1890. (LCHS No. 1007.)

Early attention was given to providing activities for young people, including visitors. George Williams's skating rink in South Beach was a popular spot. This photograph was taken May 28, 1887. (LCHS No. 1904.)

Sam Case came to the Coast Reservation as a volunteer soldier in 1861. He stayed as an agency farmer, supervising farming activities of the Native Americans and lobbying to open parts of the reservation to settlement. When that occurred in 1866, he claimed land at the entrance to Yaquina Bay and built the Ocean House, the area's first tourist hotel. Case is pictured with his family. His wife, Mary Craigie, was the daughter of a fur trapper and Bannock Indian chief. (LCHS No. 1757.)

The Ocean House opened on Independence Day of 1866, the year this photograph was taken. Case is pictured leaning on the lower level pillar of the Ocean House. (LCHS No. 2252.)

This photograph of the Bayfront was taken about 1877. Nothing is known about the buildings in the foreground. The building on the hill is the Ocean House, probably the first resort hotel on the entire Oregon coast. (LCHS No. 2253.)

Fred Olsson came with Capt. Solomon Dodge in 1863 to establish a base for Winant and Company's oyster harvesting business. In 1866, Olsson took up a claim of 112 acres on the northeast side of Yaquina Bay. He returned to Sweden in 1871 and came back with a bride, Anna Carlson. They built a large house and barn on the property. This view of Olssonville was taken in 1898 from the east facing west to Newport. (LCHS No. 947.)

24

Fred Olsson got into the tourist business early, clearing an area for tents and building small cottages. Memories of staying in one of the cottages and tents are recounted in a booklet, *When Time Stood Still*, by Florence Hofer Bynon. She describes the small cottage in detail. A rare interior photograph taken about 1900 of a tent shows the care given to provide comfort for visitors. (Above, LCHS No. 2063; below, LCHS No. 2254.)

John Nye claimed a parcel in what is now Nye Beach and built a cabin on the creek that was called Nye Brook. That creek now runs underground and empties into the ocean. Nye stayed 19 months, long enough to prove his claim, and then went east to marry. He platted the land then sold it in the 1880s to Sam Irvin. (LCHS No. 2255.)

Lemuel and Mary Davis established an early claim in what is now the South Beach area. Pictured in front of the house, built in 1890, are members of the Davis family. (LCHS No. 2052.)

By 1870, shipping was picking up, and a lighthouse was built to guide ships into the harbor. Yaquina Bay Lighthouse (above) was built at a cost of $24,000 but only kept in service from 1871 to 1874, when a new lighthouse was opened at Yaquina Head, a more strategic location. Yaquina Bay Lighthouse is pictured here around 1886 to 1893. Yaquina Head Lighthouse and auxiliary buildings are pictured below in the 1890s. (Above, LCHS No. 1016; below, LCHS No. 972.)

In 1881, the federal government appropriated $465,000 to build a jetty on the south side of the bay, raising prospects for shipping and fishing. This photograph was taken about 1888. (LCHS No. 1211.)

A rail line was built to carry materials during the construction of the south jetty. Workers are pictured with a locomotive on the line May 28, 1887. (LCHS No. 1902.)

The government constructed housing and other facilities for the jetty workers. Workers are shown in front of the mess hall on May 28, 1887. (LCHS No. 1903.)

Edward Seidler, a barber, saw an opportunity provided by tourists and built a bathhouse on Bay Beach, shown here behind the jetty about 1890. Later he followed the tourist trade to Nye Beach and built a bathhouse there. (LCHS No. 344.)

Cyclists traversed the beach, along with other vehicles. This photograph, taken about 1890, shows a man believed to be Newport postmaster Healy and an unidentified companion. (LCHS No. 1753.)

In 1896, the U.S. Life Saving Service, a forerunner of the Coast Guard, established a station at South Beach on Yaquina Bay. The USLSS offered demonstration drills like this one on the Bayfront in 1898, drawing large crowds. (LCHS No. 1152.)

James Winant, who harvested oysters and established Oysterville, was involved in shipping ventures as well. His ship *The Mischief* is pictured here in Yaquina Bay about 1889. (LCHS No. 1752.)

Some new towns declared themselves to be "dry," meaning no liquor could be sold. Newport was not one. By 1867, Newport already had two saloons. When railroad service came to Yaquina City, more saloons opened in Newport to service the additional visitors. The photograph here shows Yaquina Brewery near Oysterville in 1882. (LCHS No. 2256.)

Dr. F. M. Carter taught the first public school in Newport in 1872. He is shown in 1913 at an Independence Day celebration years after he stopped teaching. Newport's first grade school is pictured below in 1885. Note that many of the children are barefoot. (Above, LCHS No. 2257; below, LCHS No. 2258.)

Col. T. Egenton Hogg and other investors incorporated the Corvallis and Yaquina Bay Railroad in October 1872. In 1874, Hogg's company became Willamette Valley and Coast Railroad Company. The State of Oregon granted the company all the marsh and tidelands in Benton County, which included much of Yaquina Bay and exempted the company from taxes for 20 years. The railroad made its first official trip in December 1884. This photograph shows a group of railroad workers around 1900. Railroad construction and maintenance brought Chinese workers to the area. (LCHS No. 2259.)

Yaquina City (located where Sawyer's Landing is now) was built in 1876 as a terminus for the railroad on land owned by the railroad. The logical terminus for the railroad was the growing town of Newport, but Newport landowners had refused $50,000 for land to bring the railroad to their town. The railroad's first big tourist trip to the coast was on July 4, 1885. The 70 passengers, in good humor, took off from Corvallis at 7:00 a.m. The trip back was difficult, with bad weather and tired passengers. Some probably had imbibed while in Newport since most Willamette Valley towns and Yaquina City were dry, although there was a saloon anchored offshore in Yaquina City, visible in this 1885 photograph. (LCHS No. 1460.)

The Yaquina City Hotel was completed in 1885 to house the people coming to and from the bay. At one time, Yaquina City was larger than Newport, with its own school, stores, and other amenities. After passenger service stopped, the town gradually faded. A 1901 fire lent a devastating blow. Passenger service was terminated in 1932. (LCHS No. 1561.)

Hogg and his investors for the railroad venture were plagued with disaster, including this 1895 wreck. The photograph shows the wreckage and two of the people killed. (LCHS No. 2260.)

Hogg and his investors expanded their shipping ventures, first with the *Yaquina City* (above), which wrecked in 1887, and then with the *Yaquina Bay*, which wrecked in 1888 (below). The *Yaquina City* carried 300 tons of wheat grown in the Willamette Valley. (Above, LCHS No. 2261; below, LCHS No. 2217.)

One of the first stores on Yaquina Bay was opened by C. H. Williams around 1877. He combined the store with a saloon operating next door. One of the attractions for visitors to Newport was the availability of liquor. (LCHS No. 1206.)

Newspapers came early to the settlements on Yaquina Bay. By 1882, when Newport incorporated, several newspapers were in print. The *Yaquina Bay News* began in 1893 and its building is pictured here around 1895. (LCHS No. 1636.)

As parts of the Coast Reservation opened to settlement, they were incorporated into Benton and Tillamook Counties. In 1893, lawyer Ben Jones was 35 years old and fed up with bad roads and the indifference of the county seat to coastal needs. He headed a delegation to the county seat at Corvallis to request 3,000 feet of lumber for road improvements. He was told that the people on the coast were a "bunch of clam diggers" who did not need roads. Jones replied, "With the cooperation of the balance of the clam diggers, we are going to create a new county." With some clever political manipulation by Jones and his allies, the Oregon Legislature approved the new county. To garner one legislator's vote, Jones agreed to name the county Lincoln County after Abraham Lincoln. Jones was appointed the first county clerk and is shown here in a portrait and in the clerk's office in Toledo (third gentleman from the left), which was named the temporary and then permanent county seat. Newport was smaller than Toledo at the time. Jones is known as the father of the county. He also was a leader in improving roads and securing funds for the Roosevelt Military Highway (now Highway 101). The bridge over Rocky Creek is named for him. (Above, LCHS No. 2262; right, LCHS No. 2330.)

When Newport incorporated in 1882, the city council's first action was to order construction of a wooden bulkhead along the bay in front of the town. A small shed-like jail was built for $38.31, including a bed and two blankets. The jail is in the upper right part of the photograph, looking small next to a two-story building. This photograph of the Bayfront was taken in the late 1800s. Newport's population in 1880 was 269. By 1890, it had grown to 1,159. (LCHS No. 2263.)

This view from the bulkhead shows the small building that was the jail more clearly. (LCHS No. 955.)

Rev. Charles Booth moved to Newport in 1886 as the permanent missionary for the Episcopal Church. On June 25, 1887, the cornerstone was laid in Newport for St. Stephens Episcopal Church, the first church erected in Newport. The church was built on the Fall Street bluff overlooking the bay. A cottage for the family was built next to it. The building was moved to Brook Street, where it has served a number of purposes up to today. Reverend Booth is shown here with his family around 1892. (LCHS No. 2203.)

There was no shortage of activities on the coast for children. They played in the sand and waves, dug for clams, improvised plays and songfests, and engaged in numerous other activities. This photograph was taken about 1900. (LCHS No. 1138, No. 2265.)

Clambakes were a popular attraction for visitors. A long wooden table was covered with clams, and people indulged. The clambakes pictured are on Bay Beach sometime between 1889 and 1896. (Above, LCHS No. 2264; below, LCHS No. 1731.)

# Three

# A NEW CENTURY

As the 1900s dawned, the Yaquina Bay area was growing, with tourism and shipping as the leading ventures. The area's fishing business also experienced a boom, followed by some busts, as newfound halibut beds were fished out. Ships carried goods to Portland and south along the coast. Tourists who had focused on the Bayfront were being lured to the beachfront, and a wooden walkway was built to connect the two areas. Entrepreneurs began to take advantage of the flow and opened homes and businesses along the walkway.

Newport, which referred to the Bayfront area at the time, had incorporated in 1882, and businesses were doing well. They suffered a setback when a fire destroyed a major retail block in 1908. As a result, a new combination city hall and fire department was built on the Bayfront. Electricity came to the area about the same time. The Ocean House had expanded to accommodate more travelers to the area, and there were several other lodging establishments there, including the Bay View House and the Copeland Rooms. The biggest addition to the Bayfront was the new three-story Abbey Hotel, built in 1911.

Possibly the earliest attraction built on Nye Beach was Dr. Minthorn's Hot Sea Baths, which opened in 1902. Many early beachgoers stayed in tents and cabins. Developer Sam Irvin built an extension to his home and converted it to a hotel in 1905. Nearby he built a log cabin recreation hall. The biggest boom came in 1912 when the Natatorium (which included a dance hall, theater, bowling alley, and swimming pool), the New Cliff House (now the Sylvia Beach Hotel), and the Nicolai Hotel opened.

Land transportation was still difficult for those early residents and tourists. Even though automobiles were becoming more common, the ocean was the main north and south route, and roads were muddy and unstable. A group of people from the Commercial Club (a forerunner of the Greater Newport Chamber of Commerce) set out to demonstrate the problem by taking a photo-documented trip from Newport to Siletz Bay, requiring 22-plus hours round-trip and the many tools they took along.

Transportation has always been a problem on the coast. At the start of the 20th century, the ocean was still the main north and south highway. Lee Doty's stage, shown here in 1917, ran between South Beach and Waldport. Four horses made travel easier, but with no cover from the weather, the passengers had to be dressed warmly. Stage operators had to pay close attention to tides and weather. (LCHS No. 1540.)

Special excursion stages, like this one on Nye Beach around 1905, took tourists to various spots to hunt for agates or see the sights. (LCHS No. 316.)

Gov. Oswald West traveled to Newport in June 1912 and spoke in front of the Abbey Hotel on the Bayfront and the Nicolai Hotel on Nye Beach, where he also attended a horse race. West is in the middle of the photograph (at right) taken on Nye Beach. About seven months later, West wrote a concise 60-word bill declaring the Oregon seashore a public highway. He proposed the bill knowing a real road would eventually replace the beach. He also knew that once the state had control of the beaches, they would not go back into private ownership. West's bill passed, giving Oregon the legacy of open public beaches. (Above, LCHS No. 2266; right, LCHS No. 1545.)

The age of the automobile arrived in the early 1900s, but the coast had no roads equipped to handle the new vehicles. The Commercial Club (a forerunner of the Greater Newport Chamber of Commerce) was fully aware of the impact of this on their future development. In 1912, William Burton organized the first automobile trip from Newport to Siletz Bay, a distance of 46.6 miles round-trip, to demonstrate to politicians the sad state of coastal transportation. He took with him a newspaper reporter and a photographer. A Studebaker dealer supplied a Flanders 20 automobile. The trip took 22 hours and 40 minutes and required every tool they had with them. In the photograph above, the travelers are descending onto the beach at a spot known as Jump-Off Joe, so named because vehicles "jumped off" the road onto the beach at that point. Below, they struggle to get their car over a sandy, treacherous spot. (Above, LCHS No. 1823; below, LCHS No. 236.)

In 1910, when this bridge over Rocky Creek was built, travel was difficult. Most large rivers and bays did not have bridges spanning them, and ferries were common. (LCHS No. 1365.)

This 1915 Nye Beach scene shows horses on the beach and, in the far background, two cars. Visible in the photograph are the Nicolai Hotel, the Natatorium, Minthorn's Hot Sea Baths, and the New Cliff House, now the Sylvia Beach Hotel. (LCHS No. 1355.)

Road building brought work to the coast. Often entire families worked on the crew, with the women and children cooking and taking care of the campsite. This photograph shows the Grant family building a road near Harlan in 1911. (LCHS No. 2168.)

Tourists hang out the windows of a Sunday excursion train from Corvallis to Yaquina City about 1905. The train did not come all the way to Newport because of a dispute with the property owners along the proposed route. The developers built Yaquina City on land they owned between Toledo and Newport. (LCHS No. 1560.)

On January 1, 1908, a fire broke out on the Bayfront. It destroyed an entire block of buildings on Front Street. By demolishing two buildings to create a firebreak, community members were able to save the rest of the town. Buildings destroyed included the Cozy Corner Shop, Stocker's Meat Market, Lee Williams's grocery store, the Keystone (soda fountain), A. D. Schollenburg's building with H. F. Jenkins jewelry and millinery store, and Booth's jewelry store. The damage was estimated at $20,000. (Above, LCHS No. 943; below, LCHS No. 942.)

Seven months after the Bayfront fire in 1908, the block was filled with new buildings. The abandoned Independent Order of the Odd Fellows building was floated down from Olssonville to the block and remains there today with the date "1895" and "IOOF" prominently remaining on the structure. A new combination city hall and fire department was built on the Bayfront that year and is visible in the lower left-hand side of the 1911 and 1912 photographs of the area. (Above, LCHS No. 935; below, LCHS No. 2165.)

Mary and Royal Bensell were prominent people in Newport. Royal came to the Coast Reservation as a volunteer soldier in 1861 and stayed to open the first sawmill. Mary was the first white woman to live on Yaquina Bay. She divorced her first husband, who was abusive, and took a job cooking for the workers at Royal Bensell's sawmill. They were married in 1868. He was a jack-of-all-trades, serving as a legislator and customs officer, writing for the *Corvallis Gazette*, doing public relations for the railroad, building boats, and engaging in real estate and development. He was mayor of Newport during the 1908 fire, presiding over the reconstruction of the area and the building of a new city hall and fire department, as well as the introduction of electricity and water. (LCHS No. 1825.)

The Bensells built a house in the 1880s just above Front Street (shown far left in this 1910s photograph), where it remains today. In the lower right-hand corner, a part of the Newport Opera House is pictured. It was the site of a variety of entertainment for the locals and visitors. For evening events, residents would take up a collection to keep the electricity on later. (LCHS No. 1402.)

The Ocean House was enlarged in the late 1880s to accommodate the increased number of visitors the railroad brought to Newport. It is shown here in both an east-facing view and from the west. The Coast Guard station is now located on the site. (Above, LCHS No. 1972; below, LCHS No. 2267.)

Clarinda Copeland (far left) stands outside her boardinghouse on the Bayfront and is seated inside at a desk in the photograph below. Clarinda came to the Coast Reservation with her husband, James Chambers, who was named trader at the store at Siletz. In 1882, James died, leaving Clarinda with four children, debts, and the store. She applied for and was granted a license to be the post trader. She was the first woman ever to receive such a license. In 1888, Clarinda married Clark Copeland. They homesteaded land east of Toledo, but Clarinda continued to enjoy business and managed a boardinghouse and a store. (Above, LCHS No. 2268; below, LCHS No. 1624.)

The arrival of the ferry was the busiest time of the day, as visitors and locals both came out for mail and to greet the newly arrived passengers. In the photograph above, the ferry *Newport* is arriving around 1914. In the photograph below, the steamer *T. M. Richardson* is shown with the band playing to greet new arrivals. (Above, LCHS No. 1562; below, LCHS No. 1317.)

Peter and Cerena Abbey played a prominent role in the development of the Bayfront. They built the second lodging facility on the Bayfront, the Bay View. It was lost to debt, so the Abbeys moved across the street and opened the Abbey House, then repurchased the old Bay View and constructed the Abbey Hotel on the grounds in 1911. (LCHS No. 1764.)

Employees of the Abbey Hotel stand on the balcony waiting with the crowd for the ferry's arrival around 1915. (LCHS No. 1563.)

Built in 1911 for $53,000, the new Abbey Hotel was three stories high and had 150 rooms and 50 baths. Much of the lumber used was from the old Yaquina City Hotel. It was floated down to the Bayfront. (LCHS No. 2269.)

The Abbey dining room was 40 by 80 feet. Guests could stay at the hotel, all-you-could-eat meals included, for $2 to $3 a night. (LCHS No. 2270.)

Fred Olsson's claim became the town of Olssonville, adjacent to Newport. As Newport grew, towns around it became part of the city of Newport. Olsson donated part of his land to the city. In the background of this 1908 photograph of Olssonville is a home built in 1890 by Dr. James R. Bayley. The home is shown from the west in the other photograph. The Bayley house burned in 1923, except for the fireplace and foundation. Gen. Ulysses Grant McAlexander built on the site in 1925. That building, with the additions made to it over the years, is scheduled to become the Pacific Maritime and Heritage Center of the Lincoln County Historical Society. (Above, LCHS No. 2271; below, LCHS No. 1137.)

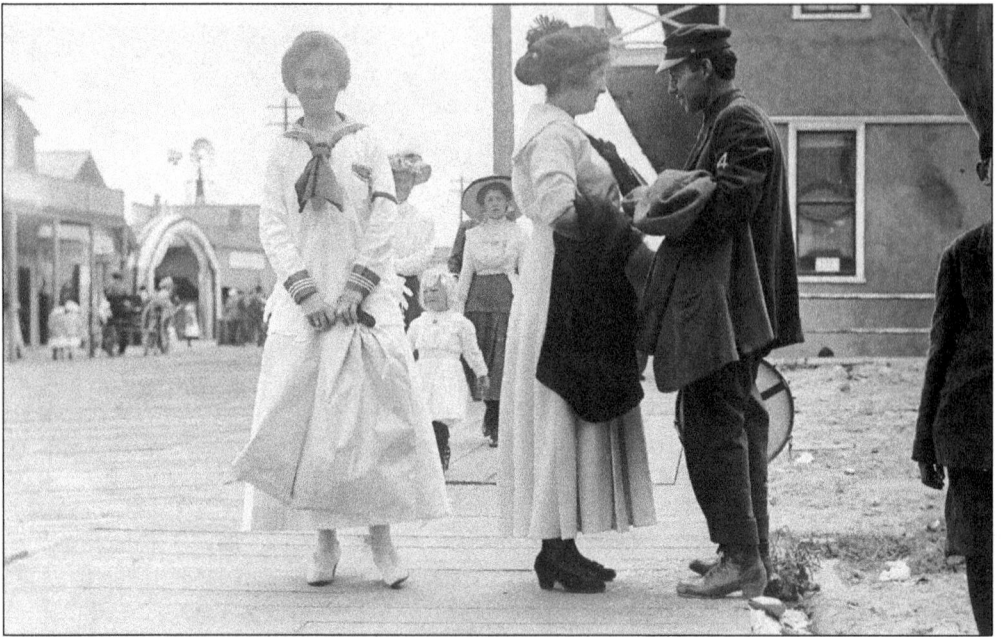

In 1912, the streets of Newport were planked to help automobiles and other vehicles avoid the muddy ruts and bumps of the dirt roads. Both photographs show the planked streets. The two people facing each other above are Marge Ingals, descendant of Newport founder Sam Case, and Rich Chatterton of the U.S. Life Saving Service. (Above, LCHS No. 1754; below, LCHS No. 937.)

The Bayfront was the site of the main post office until 1912, when a new one opened midway between the Bayfront and Nye Beach. The post office is shown around 1910. (LCHS No. 2272.)

The first bank of Newport, Western State Bank, opened on the Bayfront in 1912. The bank is shown about that time. (LCHS No. 2273.)

Visitors and locals could spiff up their shoes at the Newport Shining Parlor for "Ladies and Gents," shown here around 1918. (LCHS No. 2274.)

Blower Brothers Market, seen here around 1911, sold fresh meat to customers in a shop next to the Abbey Hotel. (LCHS No. 2275.)

Charles L. Kisor was the proprietor of Newport Cleaning and Pressing Parlor, located on the Bayfront. The exterior photograph was taken about 1910, the interior about 1915. (Above, LCHS No. 2276; below, LCHS No. 2277.)

The Newport Band played at celebrations and other events. This photograph was taken about 1911 and includes, from left to right, Lyle Lewis, Edgar George, Lloyd Collver, Ray Collver, ? Bartlett, Cecil Berry, unidentified, Virgil Rich, Paul Smith, Ralph Collver, and Lloyd Blakely. (LCHS No. 2279.)

Independence Day in 1911 was celebrated with a parade on the Bayfront. (LCHS No. 2280.)

Memorial services honoring those who died and were lost at sea were commonly held on the bay. (LCHS No. 2278.)

Memorial Day was also called Decoration Day because many people decorated the graves of the dead. This photograph shows a Memorial Day commemoration at Eureka Cemetery on May 30, 1912. (LCHS No. 2066.)

Commercial and recreational fishing were both big businesses on the Bayfront. This photograph shows a *c.* 1910 catch of rockfish. (LCHS No. 1347.)

Abundant halibut beds were discovered off the coast of Newport in 1912. This photograph shows a catch from the *Ollie S.* in that year. The halibut banks soon were fished out. (LCHS No. 2164.)

Mike Jacobson (behind the child in front) became a ferry boat captain like his father, Capt. O. F. (Oscar) Jacobson, who was a member of the U.S. Life Saving Service and also captain of several ferry boats in Newport. Mike also ran the ferry *Sadie B* in the 1930s. (LCHS No. 785.)

Mac Hofer and Sabine Dent, summer visitors to Newport, later married and spent their honeymoon in Newport. The photograph was taken near Olssonville in 1903. (LCHS No. 1404.)

Just before World War I, the Bayfront was a busy place. (LCHS No. 951.)

This 61-pound chinook salmon was almost as big as the man who caught it. (LCHS No. 1810.)

As visitors began to discover the pleasures of the ocean beaches, Newport built a planked walkway from the Bayfront to Nye Beach. The hike over the hill was hard, but people walked the path cheerfully, as the photographs illustrate. The photograph above shows a genial group from the Bayfront side. The photograph below shows Fall Street from near the top of the hill. (Above, LCHS No. 1318; below, LCHS No. 1985.)

Sixth Street, the main north and south street on the hill between the Bayfront and the oceanfront, was a mix of residential and commercial buildings. In the photograph above, a parade winds down the street. About 1912, a new building on Sixth Street became the post office on the lower level and home of the Independent Order of Odd Fellows on the top floor (photograph below). That building now houses a restaurant and other retail businesses. (Above, LCHS No. 1657; below, LCHS No. 1656.)

Elmer Patrick also recognized the value of being between the Bayfront and the ocean. He built a grocery store on the way up the hill from the Bayfront. The building still stands. Through the years it has been an armory, funeral home, telephone and telegraph office, and radio station. A Presbyterian church (now the Calvary Baptist Church on Ninth and Alder Streets) became part of the growing midway also. (Above, LCHS No. 2281; right, LCHS No. 1014.)

Theresa and Charles Roper moved to Newport to open a photography studio. In 1913, they built their home to look like a Welsh castle and referred to it as Highland (or Hilan) Castle. The boardwalk between the Bayfront and beach ran right past, bringing a steady stream of customers to their studio. (LCHS No. 2282.)

Constructed in 1895 by John and Susan Burrows, the building in this photograph now houses a museum administered by the Lincoln County Historical Society. John and Susan were divorced shortly after their marriage, and Susan operated the home as a boardinghouse until 1914. Three families operated funeral homes out of the property, the last being the Batemans. It was purchased in 1976 by the Bank of Newport and donated to the society, which moved it from Highway 101 to its current location on Ninth Street. (LCHS No. 1309.)

A grade school occupied this building until Central Grade School was constructed in 1936 by the Works Progress Administration. Newport grade school was expanded to accommodate the higher grades, and upper level classes were held there until May 1914. In 1914, a new high school was built where the Lincoln County courthouse now stands. (LCHS No. 261.)

In the fall of 1914, high school students moved into a new school on Olive Street, midway between the Bayfront and Nye Beach, where the county courthouse is now located. (LCHS No. 2283.)

The Bayfront developed earlier than the ocean beach areas, but ocean beaches were popular spots for camping. The families of Copeland and Chambers took time away from their Siletz and Toledo homes to camp at Nye Beach in this c. 1892 photograph. (LCHS No. 312.)

In 1893, a stock market panic ushered in the worst economic depression of that century. It was in those dark days that John Fitzpatrick established the Monterey Hotel, the biggest, grandest resort hotel on the central Oregon coast, near Agate Beach. Fitzpatrick died a year or two after the hotel was built, and his wife and children continued to run it. However, the depression and the hotel's location isolated it from the Bayfront and Nye Beach, leading to economic problems for the family. (LCHS No. 2284.)

Sam Irvin was an educator and became a developer and strong advocate for the Newport and Nye Beach areas. He purchased land in Nye Beach from John Nye and R. M. Thompson and sold plats there. He was instrumental in bringing the Summer Education Association to Nye Beach in 1898. He also tried to get a state teachers college for the area. (LCHS No. 1013.)

Dr. Thomas Condon, a leading Oregon educator, taught most of his geology classes for the Summer Education Association outside, as seen in this 1898 photograph of a group of students at Nye Beach. (LCHS No. 1559.)

Sam Irvin built his home just off Agnes (now Third) Street in Nye Beach. The expanded building later became the Irvin Hotel. Nearby he constructed a log cabin recreation hall. Fashioned after a building at the Lewis and Clark Expo of 1905 in Portland, the structure featured a bowling alley and dance hall. The Irvin Hotel was sold to John Kelly in 1913 and became the Kelly Hotel. For a while, the building served as Newport's first hospital. (Above, LCHS No. 2285; below, LCHS No. 1766.)

As Nye Beach grew in popularity, people gathered on the beach to wade, sunbathe, and enjoy each other's company. (LCHS No. 925.)

Edward Seidler, a barber by trade, had a bathhouse near the north jetty and saw advantages to building one at Nye Beach also. Edward and son Albert are on the roof of the Nye Beach bathhouse hanging rented bathing suits to dry. (LCHS No. 2286.)

Another early-20th-century Nye Beach building served a number of purposes, including rooms for rent, a restaurant, and offices. Located at the corner of Agnes (now Third) and Coast Streets, it stretched to Beach Street and was home at one time or another to the Osburn Hotel, the Nyebrook Hotel, the Saunders Hotel, and other businesses. At one time, L. C. Smith had an office in the building. Smith was a Nye Beach developer who sold lots and called the area "The Promised Land," promising that one day the area would be part of the town of Newport. The building was demolished in a controlled burn in 1959. (LCHS No. 1980.)

Photographer A. L. Thomas moved to Nye Beach in 1895 and ran an agate and curio shop and sold many of his photographs as postcards. He built this shop and a lavish home in the early 1900s. He also had the first rock-cutting and polishing shop in the United States and used bicycle pedals to power the polisher. (LCHS No. 2287.)

74

The planked walkway from the Bayfront followed Agnes (now Third) Street to Nye Beach. Houses lined the walkway, and riders followed along the side of the planked walkway. (Above, LCHS No. 1532; below, LCHS No. 1520.)

One of the more extravagant facilities in Nye Beach was Dr. Minthorn's Hot Sea Baths (on the hill to the right in the photograph). Minthorn, who believed in the recuperative powers of soaking in hot seawater, built the three-story facility on Nye Beach in 1902. The higher up the guest area, the more expensive the treatment was. On the left in the photograph is the Natatorium, built in 1911. It featured a theater, dance hall, bowling alley, and swimming pool. Until a renovation in the later 1930s, the pool was heated salt water. (LCHS No. 305.)

The small building on the right offered a place to change into beach clothes, warm up by the fireplace, and get a snack. The building remains and is owned and used by the Yaquina Art Association. (LCHS No. 318.)

The New Cliff House was built in 1912 by Wilson D. Wheeler. It was adjacent to Minthorn's Hot Sea Baths on Nye Beach. The building remains and is operated as the Sylvia Beach Hotel, which is on the National Register of Historic Places. (LCHS No. 151.)

The Nicolai Hotel opened in 1912 on Nye Beach. The grand opening was the social event of the season. Gov. Oswald West was on hand for the ceremonies. The Nicolai was the most expensive hotel in Newport, but it was never a commercial success and, on occasion, took a beating from the ocean. It was torn down in 1933. (LCHS No. 2288.)

By 1914, Nye Beach was crowded with tourist attractions. This view from the southwest shows, from left to right, the Nicolai Hotel, the Natatorium, the bathhouse, Minthorn's Hot Sea Baths, and the New Cliff House. (LCHS No. 1567.)

Sumner Hitchings and his wife operated a cigar factory on the corner of Brook and Olive Streets in Nye Beach. Their son, Edward, is on the roof. (LCHS No. 1874.)

Jump-Off Joe, shown in the 1880s, was a popular rock formation on Nye Beach. Gradually the formation eroded until it disappeared in 1916. (LCHS No. 500.)

By 1914, Jump-Off Joe had broken away from the shoreline and eroded considerably. (LCHC No. 2289.)

By early 1916, Jump-Off Joe had eroded more. To the right, another formation known as Slipper Rock is visible. (LCHS No. 304.)

By late 1916, the arch of Jump-Off Joe collapsed. (LCHS No. 2290.)

The main attraction at Nye Beach was the beach itself. Bathing beauties came in a variety of garments to enjoy the surf. (Above, LCHS No. 929; right, LCHS No. 917.)

Patrick's Grocery was an early addition to Nye Beach. Beach Street is still the main street leading to the ocean. (LCHS No. 1329.)

There were several agate shops in Nye Beach, including Ruddiman's (shown here), located in the back of the Natatorium. (LCHS No. 2291.)

At the start of the 20th century, people still prospected for gold, as shown in this photograph of a gold sluice on Nye Beach. (LCHS No. 1207.)

SCENE AT AGATE BEACH - ORE.

Agate Beach evolved when a surge of development also was taking place at Nye Beach. This scene shows Agate Beach during that era in the 1910s. (LCHS No. 2292.)

Agate Beach, north of Nye Beach, developed on land originally owned by George and Julia Megginson. Julia, a Siletz Indian, is shown here in front of their house. (LCHS No. 396.)

This Agate Beach building housed a small restaurant and an office for development. (LCHS No. 2293.)

The Agate Beach Inn was one of the first buildings constructed in the development. The post office is shown on the right. (LCHS No. 2294.)

The Agate Beach area was popular with early surfers, some pictured in this c. 1913 photograph. (LCHS No. 133.)

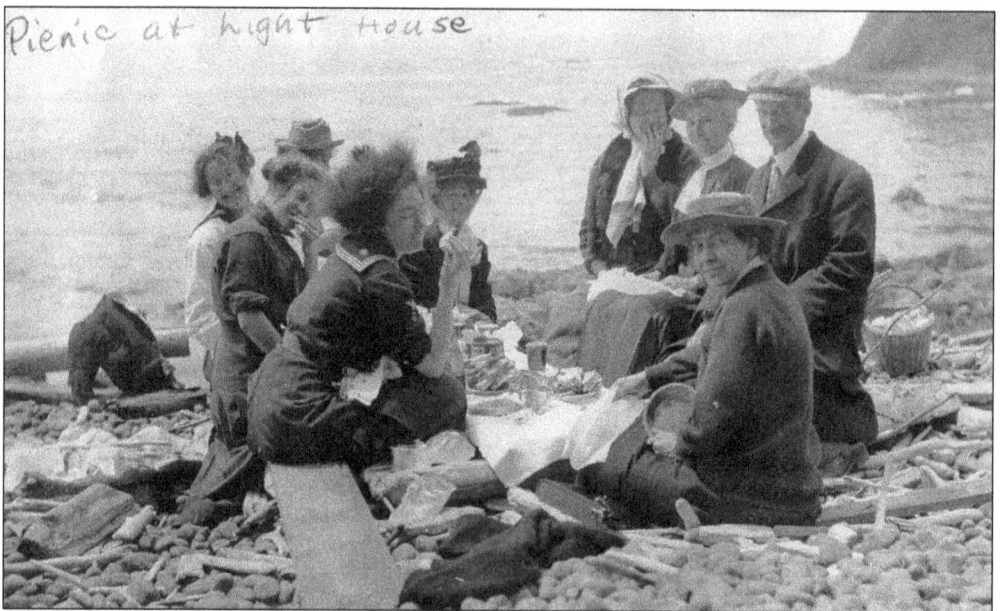

Picnic at Light House

Picnics on the beach were popular. This group enjoys one at Agate Beach below Yaquina Head Lighthouse around 1915. (LCHS No. 240.)

The U.S. Life Saving Service, a forerunner of the Coast Guard, established a station at South Beach about 2 miles south of Yaquina Bay. It operated there until 1906. (LCHS No. 2295.)

Several buildings made up the South Beach station of the U.S. Life Saving Service, including lodging for the crew. (LCHS No. 2296.)

The U.S. Life Saving Service is launching from their South Beach location in this photograph. (LCHS No. 1151.)

The South Beach location was not ideal for sighting ships in danger, and lifesavers had to patrol the beach nightly. When the U.S. Life Saving Service moved into the decommissioned Yaquina Bay Lighthouse in 1906, patrols became unnecessary. In 1915, the USLSS became the Coast Guard and continued to operate out of the lighthouse until 1932. (LCHS No. 1153.)

In the early 1900s, Yaquina Head Lighthouse had several buildings, as well as the garden shown in the forefront of this photograph. Yaquina Head sometimes was wrongly referred to as Cape Foulweather. (LCHS No. 2069.)

# Four

# WARS, DEPRESSION, AND RECOVERY

When the United States entered World War I in 1917, the central Oregon coast had just gone through a time of growth, with new hotels and tourist facilities and improvements for residents. The war would change the coast in many ways but most dramatically by the arrival of the Spruce Production Division of the U.S. Army, which was to boost the nation's production of Sitka spruce lumber for construction of airplanes. More than 3,000 soldiers and civilian employees went to work building whatever was necessary to secure spruce for the war.

The poor state of roads in general, and the coastal highway in particular, highlighted the difficulty of moving materials and people during wartime and led to an impetus to improve conditions. The result was construction of the Roosevelt Military Highway, now known as Highway 101. Highway 20 from Corvallis to Newport also was improved.

After World War I, the population of the area increased, and people began to lead normal lives again. Nye Beach and the Bayfront continued to draw tourists, and the area midway between the two and along Sixth Street became a thriving downtown.

During the 1930s, the country was hit with a deep recession. Newport received some relief through projects funded by the National Industrial Recovery Act, including construction of Yaquina Bay Bridge, which was completed in 1936. Sixth Street was chosen as the new route to connect to the bridge, necessitating moving several buildings back to widen the street.

When World War II broke out, Newport became concerned with blackouts, rationing, the possibility of an enemy invasion on the coast, and winning the war. Some fishermen went off to fight; others turned their boats over to the military for patrolling the coast; and others fished for shark, the livers of which were fed to soldiers to improve their night vision.

After the war, the area struggled to rebuild tourism, retail, and maritime ventures. Newport became the county's largest town. It won the county seat in 1952, and a new courthouse was built in midtown.

More than 3,000 soldiers and civilians poured into Lincoln County during World War I to build the infrastructure for a massive spruce logging venture to make lightweight lumber for airplane construction. Buildings were taken over to use during the operation, including structures on the Bayfront that served as administrative offices and a drafting room. This photograph was taken around 1918. (LCHS No. 1633.)

A hospital was constructed at South Beach for soldiers who had contracted a life-threatening strain of the Spanish flu. Quarantines were placed on the spruce camps at the height of the epidemic. Medical personnel gathered for a photograph at South Beach in 1918. (LCHS No. 2297.)

The Ocean Hill Hotel (formerly the Monterey) in Agate Beach was taken over as quarters for the Spruce Division. The soldiers of the Spruce Division constructed the railroad trestle in the background. The trestle later became part of Highway 101. Tents were set up to accommodate the enlisted men, while the officers stayed in the hotel. (LCHS No. 2298.)

The Spruce Division's goal was to boost the nation's production of Sitka spruce lumber from 3 to 10 million board feet a year. Straight grain spruce is both strong and lightweight, ideal for construction of airplanes needed for the war effort. The war ended before the milling operation was completed, leaving Lincoln County with the infrastructure for a full-scale wood products industry. (LCHS No. 1476.)

The U.S. Life Saving Service ushered in the World War I era with a new motor-propelled boat. The *Undaunted* arrived at Yaquina Bay in March 1914. Built of mahogany and oak, the 36-foot, self-righting craft was equipped with a 40-horsepower gasoline engine and an electric searchlight. It was the only power rescue boat between the Columbia River and Bandon. In 1915, the USLSS was renamed the U.S. Coast Guard. (LCHS No. 1673.)

In 1932, the Coast Guard built a new station at the west end of Bay Boulevard, near the base of the hill where the current station sits. Coast Guard personnel are pictured in 1935 in front of this station. That year the Coast Guard experienced a tragedy. A crew in a 36-foot motor lifeboat responded to a distress signal from a tug towing a dredge in the Yaquina Bay channel. While the Coast Guard personnel struggled to pull a civilian from the water into their lifeboat, it was hit by a wave and capsized. Without warning, seven men, two of them civilians, found themselves in frigid water. Only two survived: Eldred Halsey and John Hart, both Coast Guard men. (The story of this event is told in *Tragedy on Yaquina Bar*, published by the Lincoln County Historical Society.) (LCHS No. 2299.)

In 1941, a substantial addition was made to the Coast Guard station on Bay Boulevard, making it one of the biggest and best-equipped stations on the Oregon coast. The station is shown here in 1943. (LCHS No. 2151.)

Disaster struck the Coast Guard station on January 4, 1944, when fire engulfed the building. Of unknown origin, the fire spread through the station rapidly on and under the first floor. The Newport Fire Department, Coast Guard personnel, and the Toledo Fire Department combined efforts to control the blaze. The station was a total loss. (LCHS No. 2300.)

The fire on January 4, 1944, left only rubble in its wake, but the motorized equipment was saved. Six barracks-type buildings were trucked in from another military installation to serve as temporary Coast Guard facilities after the fire destroyed the Bayfront facility. They were placed on land near where Newport's current hospital is located. (LCHS No. 2301.)

In 1949, a new Coast Guard facility opened on the hill above the former station. A dock was built where the former station had been. The main building and some auxiliary buildings still house today's Coast Guard. (LCHS No. 2302.)

The Coast Guard used
Yaquina Bay Lighthouse until
1932 and built a tower next
to the lighthouse. In 1948,
Miss Newport contestants
posed at the lighthouse, which
was under threat of being
demolished. (LCHS No. 967.)

Yaquina Bay Lighthouse was saved from demolition by the Lincoln County Historical Society,
which was formed in 1948. Members of the society erected a historic site marker and posed in
front of the sign in 1956. (LCHS No. 1919.)

Yaquina Head Lighthouse continued to function with a complex that included a duplex for the keeper and assistant keeper, another lodging facility, and a garden. (LCHS No. 1821.)

In 1938, the keepers' duplex was torn down. The next year the lighthouse passed into Coast Guard hands. (LCHS No. 2303.)

On August 14, 1934, construction began on Yaquina Bay Bridge. The million-dollar bridge was paid for with Works Project Administration funds and designed by Conde McCullough. More than 200 men were employed by Gilpin and General Construction Companies. The weekly payroll was as much as $5,000. Skilled positions went to electricians and ironworkers with bridge- or dam-building experience. High above Yaquina Bay, in driving wind and rain, workers risked their lives. There was one fatality. (Right, LCHS No. 1220; below, LCHS No. 1229.)

Construction began on both sides of the bay. Original survey work was incorrect on the east. If this had not been discovered, the two ends of the bridge would not have aligned. To build the bridge, 25,000 cubic yards of earth were moved, 30,000 cubic yards of concrete poured, and more than 3,000 tons of steel bolted and welded into place. Despite a thick fog, 3,000 people attended the grand opening of the Yaquina Bay Bridge on October 3, 1936. Dr. F. M. Carter was given the honor of being the first person across the bridge. The bridge made the ferry in this photograph obsolete. (LCHS No. 1689.)

Lands on the north and south ends of the bridge were acquired by the state parks board to prevent "the usual cluttering up of cheap hot dog stands and unsightly cheap eating joints that might otherwise mar the entrance to the most picturesque bridge on the Oregon Coast Highway," according to the *Yaquina Bay News* of November 2, 1934. (LCHS No. 2304.)

A locomotive sits near the bridge when work was being done on the north jetty. The tracks were laid to move materials to the jetty. (LCHS No. 1502.)

When this photograph was taken in 1947, South Beach was relatively undeveloped. (LCHS No. 1021.)

About 25,000 people came to the small town of Newport in 1938 for a free lunch. The first Crab Festival took place when tourism on the central Oregon coast was doing badly, Dungeness crab was abundant, and the price was low. Newport resident Andy Naterlin founded the festival and promoted it widely. The Crab Festival continued until 1952, with a break for World War II. The first Crab Festival queen, Maxine Omlid, and her court wore shimmering gowns reminiscent of mermaids. (LCHS No. 2305.)

Miss Newport of 1947, Helen McFetridge, was called on to help promote the Crab Festival. (LCHS No. 2007.)

During the 1947 Crab Festival, Highway 101 was covered with tourists. The building that was then city hall is seen in the photograph and today is a restaurant and offices. (LCHS No. 2306.)

Elaborate schemes were devised to promote the Crab Festival. In 1947, a Hudson sedan was given away, along with other prizes. Andy Naterlin, founder of the Crab Festival, is pictured fourth from right. Legally blind, Naterlin served the city for years and was the mayor of Newport from 1941 to 1946. He went on to serve in the Oregon State Senate from 1956 to 1968. (LCHS No. 1519.)

By the 1940s, the old Newport High School was in poor condition. Leaks were a constant problem, and the building shook during strong winds—sometimes so bad that students were sent home. This building was torn down in the early 1950s when a new high school was constructed. The county courthouse now stands at this site. (LCHS No. 2307.)

The Newport Junior High girls' basketball team posed in front of the old high school in 1930. (LCHS No. 2173.)

Students work in the old high school library in 1948. (LCHS No. 2308.)

A new high school was built in the early 1950s in Newport. Pictured here in 1958, it is still in use. (LCHS No. 2309.)

Central Elementary School was built in 1935 and 1936 with Works Progress Administration funds. In 1976, it was converted to a community and senior center. The building was completely renovated to become city hall in 2002. (LCHS No. 2310.)

Esther Copeland was a member of the first graduating class of Toledo High School. She began her teaching career right out of college but was required by the school board to stop teaching when she married Maurice Andersen, as married women were not allowed to teach. During World War II, she taught again because of a shortage of male teachers. Esther became a member of the school board and worked to allow married women to teach. Esther was also the first woman to vote in Lincoln County. She is pictured here with her first-grade class at Central Elementary School around 1950. Esther retired from Central in 1956. (LCHS No. 2311.)

World War I brought America out of isolation. Here on the coast, it demonstrated that the poor roads could not support the movement of people and materials north and south. Locals and others petitioned to have the highways improved, and funds were allocated for the Roosevelt Military Highway (now Highway 101), which was named after Pres. Theodore Roosevelt. This photograph shows construction on the Roosevelt Military Highway at South Beach in 1929. (LCHS No. 2312.)

Sixth Street in Newport's city center was chosen as the new route for the Roosevelt Military Highway construction, creating upheaval that included moving some buildings out of the path of the road. Sixth Street was chosen, partly to line up with the new bridge being constructed. This photograph was taken about 1935. (LCHS No. 2313.)

Siletz mail stage on Toledo Newport highway near Toledo

The Toledo-to-Newport road, now part of Highway 20, was muddy most of the year and almost impossible to travel. In this photograph, horses and a cart are bogged down. Nearby planks help little to make the road passable. (LCHS No. 2314.)

In 1952, the state provided $1.5 million to build four bridges and a new route just south of the old Toledo-to-Newport road. By then, the route had been designated Highway 20, the culmination of a cross-country highway. This photograph shows construction on Highway 20 in 1952. (LCHS No. 2315.)

Throughout the history of Newport, the Bayfront has had an active shipping and fishing industry. In this September 1945 photograph, the fishing fleet is docked east of the bridge. (LCHS No. 1991.)

The *Mystic*, with owner Herman Kruger and crew, go out to sea in April 1946. (LCHS No. 1141.)

A crew member unloads salmon after a good day's catch around 1949. (LCHS No. 1344.)

In the fall of 1949, the Yaquina Dock and Dredge Company opened an international dock at McLean Point. The dock was made from two surplus World War II navy ships that were purchased from the government and sunk. The *Falkanger* was the first ship to dock at McLean Point. She was loaded with a quarter of a million feet of railroad ties and sailed the same day, November 17, 1949. (LCHS No. 1144.)

Outport Stevedores, Inc., a union for dockworkers, established a branch in Newport about 1947, when this photograph was taken. One day in 1952, three ships arrived and docked in Newport on Yaquina Bay for shipments of lumber. Shipping was so heavy that a competing dock was built at McLean Point. Once this dock was operational, another union, the Independent Stevedores of Coos Bay, also set up shop in Newport. The longshoremen wages were considered very high for the time. (LCHS No. 2316.)

Jens Steenson, driver for Newport Spruce Company, waited in line on the Bayfront with a spruce log to be dumped into the water and floated to a mill in August 1939. (LCHS No. 2143.)

The *Seamar* unloads lumber from "dolphins" (small flat vessels) at Johnson's South Beach dock built in 1947. The lumber is from the C. D. Johnson Lumber Mill in Toledo at Yaquina Bay. The public crabbing dock is located there now. The photograph was taken November 9, 1947. (LCHS No. 2317.)

Fishing vessels dock at Newport, which has several fish packing and canning plants visible in this August 1947 photograph. (LCHS No. 1993.)

Mo Niemi and the restaurants she started are an institution on the Oregon coast. The original Mo's is located at 622 Southwest Bay Boulevard. Mo and a partner bought the building in 1942 when it was operating as Good Eats Café. By 1946, Mo was the sole owner. In the 1960s, a woman drove her car through the front of the building. Mo replaced the window with a garage door, with a painting on the inside of the surprised woman at the wheel of her car. (LCHS No. 2335.)

People gather for a Christmas parade on the Bayfront. One decorated truck is visible in this c. 1950 photograph. The Fisherman's Wharf building is still on the Bayfront. Today a second Mo's Restaurant is located in this building. (LCHS No. 2318.)

When Sixth Street was chosen as the main route for the highway through Newport, the midway section solidified as the main commercial area. The theater and IOOF buildings remain, as well as some of the other structures now occupied with other businesses. The movie on the marquee in the photograph is *The Lost Weekend*, starring Ray Milland and Jane Wyman, distributed in 1945. (LCHS No. 999.)

Construction for a hospital at the current site began in 1951, and the grand opening of Pacific Communities Hospital was held in 1952. Until the new hospital was built, Newport was served by Pacific View Hospital, which consisted of two frame houses joined by a walkway in the Nye Beach area. Major surgery was done at Toledo's hospital. Pacific Communities Hospital Association, which was formed in 1948, raised the $121,000 needed to get federal funds to construct the hospital. (LCHS No. 2319.)

Voters chose Newport to replace Toledo as the county seat in a 1952 election. Voters also approved $400,000 to build a new courthouse. The facility was dedicated in 1955. Changes were made to the building in 1963 and 1993. Businesses, like Penneys, followed the lead by also relocating from Toledo to Newport. (LCHS No. 2075.)

Newport City Hall, located at the intersection of Coast Highway and Alder Street, was dedicated December 30, 1925. It replaced an aging 1908 city hall on the Bayfront. In a special election, the citizens of Newport voted to "erect, equip, and maintain a building to be used as city hall, public library, fire and police station." The City of Newport moved out of this building and into the Naterlin Center (formerly Central Grade School) in August 2002. (LCHS No. 1652.)

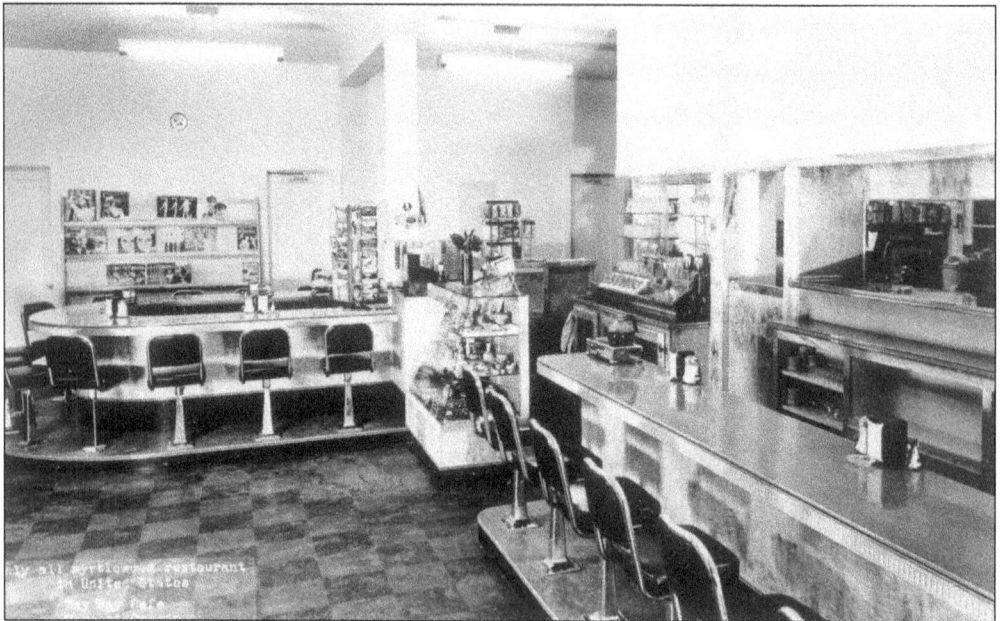

The Bay Way Café, located in the midway area in the 1940s, was also the location of the bus stop. The popular café boasted that it was the only "all myrtlewood restaurant in the United States." All of the interior wood was Oregon myrtle. (LCHS No. 1255.)

With the growing popularity of automobiles, auto camps sprang up to serve the driving population. Cars could drive up to cabins and park directly by their accommodations. The small parking garages protected the automobile (many with canvas or no tops) from weather damage. Gas also was generally available at the auto camps. Roosevelt Auto Camp, pictured here, had "nine modern and two semi-modern cottages with cooking facilities, five motel rooms and eleven garages." It was located on the Roosevelt Military Highway (Highway 101) in the midtown section of Newport. (LCHS No. 2320.)

Parker Funeral Home was a prominent feature of midtown Newport in the 1940s. Built in 1895 by John and Susan Burrows, the building was a funeral home from 1933 to 1976. The last funeral home in the building was Bateman's. In 1976, the building was moved from its location on Highway 101 to Ninth Street, after which it became the Burrows House Museum operated by the Lincoln County Historical Society. (LCHS No. 1952.)

Midtown was the location of a large and popular skating rink in the 1940s. The resident instructor and professional skater, Freddy Flesher, shown here in 1949, was also an avid long board surfer, as well as a fisherman working out of Newport and Alaska. (LCHS No. 2321.)

Beach Street in Nye Beach remained the main street to the ocean in the 1920s. The Natatorium at the west end of the street is gone, but many of the other buildings remain. (LCHS No. 103.)

Until the bridge and new stretch of highway connecting to it was completed, Coast Street in Nye Beach was a main thoroughfare through Newport. Businesses, including the Union Gas Station, lined the street. (LCHS No. 102.)

One of the popular attractions in Nye Beach in the 1920s and 1930s was a miniature golf course. The course was just east of the Natatorium. (LCHS No. 1301.)

Nye Beach was a popular hangout spot for people of all ages. These young people gathered in the sand, around 1920, by a sign advertising a "Clam Bake and Jubilee." During the summer months, wooden walls were erected on the sand to protect beach visitors from the wind. (LCHS No. 314.)

Peter and Cecile Gilmore acquired the New Cliff House in 1921, trading their chicken ranch for the hotel. The Gilmore's dog, Pat, was an integral part of the hotel operation. He carried luggage, delivered papers, and provided entertainment for the guests. He also is credited with saving Cecile's life. In 1929, the Gilmore's automobile rolled on Highway 20, trapping both Peter and Cecile. The dog ran to nearby loggers for help, saving Cecile's life. (LCHS No. 352.)

"Lobby" Hotel Gilmore by The Sea, Newport, Ore.

After Peter Gilmore died in the car accident, Cecile continued operating the hotel until she sold it in 1957. The building remains, most recently operated as the Sylvia Beach Hotel, and is on the National Register of Historic Places. (LCHS No. 2326.)

One of the popular rock formations on Nye Beach in the 1930s was called Slipper Rock. It sometimes is confused with Jump-Off Joe, which collapsed much earlier, in about 1916. (LCHS No. 1359.)

The collapse of rock formations, like Jump-Off Joe and Slipper Rock, was one indication of the instability of the land in that area. Attempts to build on the nearby land have resulted in disasters, like this landslide in 1943. When the earth moved, buildings slid into the chasm. (LCHS No. 2322.)

Automobiles used the beach as a highway, as did other forms of transportation. This photograph, taken around 1930, shows a popular activity: airplane rides for a penny a pound. The death of a woman who was hit by a plane on Nye Beach might have contributed to the order prohibiting the activity in 1930. (LCHS No. 1837.)

The driver of this 1932 Chevrolet sedan parked too close to the incoming tide in September 1945. He went for a walk on the beach with friends, and when they returned, the waves were touching the wheels of the car. A tow truck from Tip Top Motors was called, but it too got stuck in the soft sand. Both vehicles were left there overnight. In the morning, kids climbed onto the top. At the next low tide, a big logging truck with a winch parked on the sand. A cable was run out to the stranded vehicles, and they were pulled onto dry sand. Both were a total loss. (LCHS No. 32.)

This photograph, taken in the late 1940s, shows that most of the buildings erected in the early 1900s remained. The Natatorium is the large building jutting out with the rounded roof. (The rounded roof replaced a peaked roof after a 1922 fire.) The small building to the right is now the home of the Yaquina Art Association. The next building in the 1940s was the Gilmore Apartments. The Gilmore Hotel (now the Sylvia Beach Hotel) is next to it. (LCHS No. 1715.)

In March 1949, a block of Beach Street in Nye Beach burned. The Pastime Tavern and Walt's Agate Shop were destroyed. At the far left is West's candy shop, and at the far right is the old theater building. Only the roof of this structure was seriously damaged. (LCHS No. 342.)

The South Beach area developed more slowly than the central part of Newport. In 1943, the City of Newport provided about 595 acres to the Civil Aeronautics Administration to build an airport for lease to the U.S. Navy during World War II. The runways and taxi system were completed, but the war ended before a base could be built, and the airport was never used by the U.S. Navy. In April 1946, the airport was returned to the city under the Surplus Property Act of 1944. The first passenger service started June 1946. This photograph shows a visit by presidential candidate Harold Stassen on May 19, 1948. (LCHS No. 2323.)

Triangle Pacific Mill operated in South Beach in the 1940s and 1950s, shutting down after a strike. The Oregon Coast Aquarium now occupies the site. The tall structure known as a wigwam burner juts up prominently. (LCHS No. 2196.)

The Agate Beach Inn continued to be a popular destination in the 1930s when this snowy image was captured. The building burned down in November 1948. (LCHS No. 2324.)

A new golf course between Agate and Monterey Beach opened for play July 1931. The original facility had a beach club with a dine-and-dance facility and an adjoining pro shop. The beach club was destroyed by fire in 1962. The current owners have owned the golf course since 1960. Newport's first golf course also was near this area, on the hillside just east of Yaquina Head Lighthouse. Exposed to wind and other adverse weather conditions, it struggled to survive. The clubhouse burned in December 1927, and the course never recovered. (LCHS No. 1030.)

Asahel Bush, a prominent newspaper owner from Salem, built this house overlooking Agate Beach as a vacation home around 1914. Ernest Bloch, an internationally known composer, was driving along the Oregon coast on his way to California in 1941 and fell in love with the area. He bought the house from the Bush family that same year. Bloch lived there with his wife, Marguerite, until his death in 1959. He composed, taught music, and held concerts in his home. (LCHS No. 1921.)

Fannie Branson was an avid horseback rider who began carving lifelike horses that eventually made her famous. She carved as a youngster but began perfecting her hobby in the mid-1930s. Fannie and her husband, Jay, moved to Agate Beach in 1949 and started a model horse museum there that year. This photograph was taken about that time. She sold her carvings to animal lovers all over the United States and in many foreign countries. Her carvings grew to between 600 and 800. Later in her life, Fannie became crippled due to complications from an accident when she was a teenager. The Lincoln County Historical Society holds a collection of Branson's horses. (LCHS No. 2325.)

Unlike World War I, when there was no imminent threat to Oregon's coast, World War II brought vigilance and blackouts. Locals signed up to volunteer in Company A, pictured here in the victory formation around 1942. (LCHS No. 1926.)

Navy blimps, like this one photographed June 3, 1945, patrolled the coast during World War II. (LCHS No. 1733.)

Soldiers on horseback patrolled the beach during World War II. (LCHS No. 1736.)

Dogs also were used to patrol the beach during World War II. (LCHS No. 1735.)

Miss Newport of 1947, Helen Elaine McFetridge, posed near the north end of the Yaquina Bay Bridge on August 17, 1947. She was named Miss Newport in July and went on to become first runner-up in the Miss Oregon pageant later that month. (LCHS No. 2014.)

Visit us at
arcadiapublishing.com

www.ingramcontent.com/pod-product-compliance
Lightning Source LLC
Chambersburg PA
CBHW050706110426

42813CB00007B/2104